Portrait of a Village

MICKLEOVER

Portrait of a Village

MICKLEOVER

Margaret Welling

The Breedon Books
Publishing Company
Derby

First published in Great Britain by
The Breedon Books Publishing Company Limited
Breedon House, 44 Friar Gate, Derby, DE1 1DA.
1997

Acknowlegements

Mrs E. Short and her family

The Monday Club members and Mrs M. McCarthy
Mrs D. Evans

Mr D. Rodgers, Managing Secretary, Mickleover
Golf Club.

ISBN 1 85983 033 1

Printed and bound by Butler & Tanner Ltd., Selwood Printing
Works, Caxton Road, Frome, Somerset.

Colour separations by Colour Services, Wigston, Leicester.

Contents

Introduction

THIS BOOKLET has been compiled from the many pictures and postcards of Mickleover collected by Bill Short. A selection from his notes for various talks have been added to give some background details.

Bill Short was a much admired, friendly man who was always prepared to support any organisation. Most of the local Senior Citizen Clubs had the benefit of his expertise.

The royalties from this book will be given to the Dr Golding Cancer Research Fund which was a charity supported by Bill during his lifetime.

Margaret Welling
January 1997

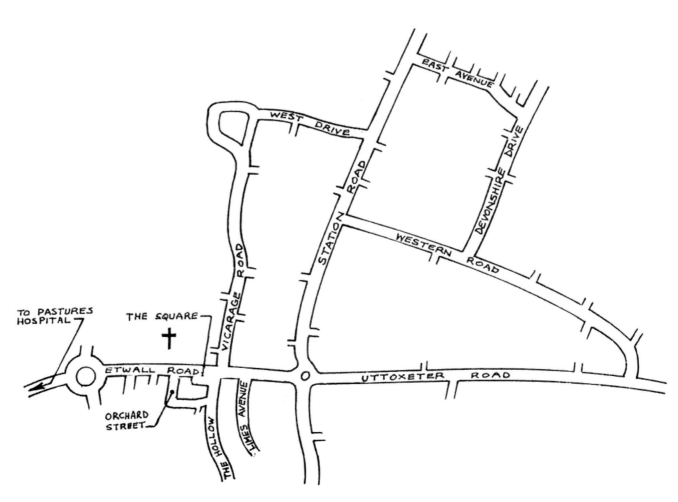

Mickleover

MICKLEOVER was first known in 1011 as Ufre (Over) which meant high ground or bank. It was called Magna Ufra in Latin documents, the Old English 'Ofer' being a slope or ridge. The prefix is thought to date from before 1087 when a nearby settlement had become established and there was a need to identify Great or Mickle Over from Little Over.

As late as 1846, Mickleover remained a small village serving the farming community with the much restored 14th-century All Saints' Church lying beside Mickleover Manor House (the Woodlands), which was built in Neo-Jacobean style for the Newton family by Duesbury in 1849.

The Newtons became the chief landowners in Mickleover until just after World War One but throughout the 19th century the Newton estate was gradually acquired by various industrialists who built their villas. The Limes, Mickleover House and Overfields were all built during the first half of the 19th century.

The area has two important timber-framed buildings, No.4 The Hollow and the Old Hall in Orchard Street, both of which date from the 17th century. The Old Hall is reputed to have been built by a captain in Cromwell's army in 1649, although the porch bears an inscription which includes in it the date 1684. The square-panelled timber frame is exposed with intermittent red brick nogging. The interior has several interesting features, notably some fine contemporary oak panelling.

One of the outstanding influences on Mickleover was undoubtedly the building of the Derbyshire Pauper Lunatic Asylum which opened in 1851 with patients coming from all over the county.

In 1895 the chairman for the hospital was Charles Edmund Newton. It can be imagined how the coming of the hospital effected the people living in the Mickleover area.

Then the Great Northern Railway came to Mickleover in 1876-77 and the village expanded with new housing. This growth continued until the outbreak of World War Two. It started again after the war when houses were being built to accommodate the overspill of people from Derby town centre which was gradually being rearranged to make way for more commerce. There were also many newcomers to the area because of the work available in local industries.

The village south of All Saints' was at one time the dominant centre core of Mickleover. When the village expanded north and east of the church, however, there seemed to develop a suburbia with no centre. In recent history, though, the building of the new St John's Church, the Church Hall, Murray Park Community School and The Robin public house, together with the nearby shops, have all been good for Mickleover.

The Square

YOU WILL NOTICE from these early pictures that The Square was originally called The Market Place. The eight pictures here show the changes that have taken place. There used to be an Annual Fair called the Wakes which was held on The Square on the first Monday following 6 December. It was a feast day dedicated to St Nicholas, patron saint of what is now All Saints' Church.

Over the years The Square has been used for many celebrations and parades. As the centre of a farming community, the old traditions of celebrating Plough Monday and Harvest Festival took place here and were linked to the nearby church.

In the 20th century any event of public note, such as a Coronation or a Jubilee, would mean that the Market Place became the hub of the celebrations. The ending of a war was marked here, and, ironically, volunteers gathering to go to war did so in the Market Place.

When Dr Hitchman came to take charge of the Derbyshire Pauper Lunatic Asylum (known later as Pastures Hospital) in 1851, he forged many links with the village. He formed a patients' brass band which played at village fêtes and other events on the Market Place. Villagers were often invited to social events that took place at the hospital and cricket matches were arranged for the male patients to play against village teams.

The Market Place was also the 'stopping place' for some of the horse transport that journeyed to and from Derby. In 1827 a coach passed through Mickleover on its way to Newcastle-under-Lyme on Mondays, Wednesdays and Fridays, returning on the days between. It would stop at various villages en route. There were also carriers from Derby to Mickleover who left Derby at 4.00 p.m. on Tuesdays and Fridays. When motorised transport was introduced, the grass on the Market Place gave way to asphalt.

The elegant drinking fountain in the centre position in the Market Place was removed in 1932 to make room for a cast-iron switchbox for the new electric lighting. Before this time three or four gas lamps gave light to the old village. The gasworks were near the railway on the lane near what is now Etwall Garage.

In 1895 the Derby Co-operative Provident Society opened a branch in Mickleover and placed it at the heart of the village. Where the 'Co-op' once stood there are still shops but The Square itself has become just a car park and a busy one too.

The Masons Arms, which was originally built in 1724 and is probably the oldest inn in Mickleover, was extended to take in an old adjoining shop. The inn now dominates one side of The Square.

The old pump in The Square was erected in 1897 to commemorate Queen Victoria's Diamond Jubilee.

A horse and cart passes the Masons Arms. Perhaps the two gentlemen are waiting for the pub to open.

Another tranquil scene in The Square. Is that a bath chair on the corner by the new telegraph pole?

Trees on the main Derby road where there is now a row of modern shops. Just behind the telegraph pole you can just make out the old sign of the Nag's Head. The original Nag's Head is seen later when looking along Uttoxeter Road.

This picture is dated during World War One. Might there be some of these children still living in Mickleover? The Derby Co-operative employees look very smart.

Just who this group were remains a mystery but they are smartly to attention on The Square.

Looking towards Derby. Notice the wall and the tree of the old Vicarage where Curzon Court now stands. How long will this lady have to wait for her bus?

Now there is a new bus stop, a bus in the distance coming from Derby and the first signs of white lines on the road.

Uttoxeter Road

FROM THE SQUARE TO MICKLEOVER GOLF CLUB

THE FIRST Mickleover Post Office was originally established in a house just beside the Market Place and was run by a post-mistress. It also acted as an Insurance Office.

The original Nag's Head was almost next door to the old Post Office and would be where the Mickleover School of Music building stands today. There were four landlords for the Nag's Head noted in the 1800s, but Mr and Mrs Hinckley were the tenants who moved from there into the new Nag's Head in 1929.

Today, walking from The Square towards the new row of shops which are set back from the road and opposite the Community Centre, you would pass the top of Limes Avenue. The Avenue was a narrow road leading to a white house, The Limes, which was built about 1836 for a local business man, Samuel Wright, a silk throwster. It was described at that time as 'a handsome modern mansion, commanding some fine views'. Even today it is a most impressive building and has a lovely conservatory. The Limes is now a residential home. The entrance to Limes Avenue was flanked by old brick cottages which have since been removed. There is one remaining older cottage in the avenue which has been cleverly restored and is a reminder of the past.

The Community Centre which stands high above Uttoxeter Road was once the National School for Boys and Girls and was built in 1881, initially to accommodate the older children of the village. The infants remained in Fennel Street (Limes Avenue). The National School was enlarged in 1905 and the infants were transferred to the school in 1916. It was used for all age groups until 1948-50. The population growth required more accommodation and the school became a Junior and Infants School only. The older pupils were moved to new schools nearby in 1950.

The education system in Mickleover can be seen to be mirrored in many villages. A Charity School using All Saints' Church as its venue had to be moved because of vandalism within the church done by the children. Robert Newton gave £200 for a school to be built on The Green in 1784. Later, a school house was built on The Green by contributions from the vicar and principal residents. The next big educational move for the village was in 1852 when Mrs Newton built a school for 100 children in Orchard Street. The parents paid one penny per week and the schoolmaster kept this money together with contributions from the wealthier villagers. The Orchard Street School became later a coffee house and reading room and is now a private residence.

Today the Community Centre houses many activities and has a small refreshment bar staffed mainly by volunteers. Rooms are let for various functions, nursery groups, sales of all kinds and it now accommodates a Women's Institute produce market on Friday mornings. In 1996 it was voted the best community centre in Derby.

The Post Office was moved into Mr Freckleton's shop in 1910, which was just along the road from the new National School and only a short distance from the Vine Inn.

The Vine Inn is one of the four inns mentioned in *Bagshaw's Directory* of 1846. It is still a popular 'local' and in the early days was the only inn in Derbyshire with a living sign. The vine grew along the wall and over the doorway. One of the landlords at the Vine was also the village wheelwright. There was a smithy adjoining the Vine and the story is told that above the smithy there was a dressmaker's room where dresses were made for the local gentry. It must have been warm work. The Derbyshire Building Society is now on that site in a new building sympathetic to the surrounding area.

Uttoxeter Road continues after the Station Road access and there is another lovely old house hidden by the mature trees and behind the Church of Our Lady of Lourdes. This Roman Catholic church was built in two stages, the first being completed in 1970 and the second in 1975 in the grounds of Mickleover Lodge.

Mickleover Lodge was built in the 1820s for George Wade (*b.*1796). He was one of a small group of 'gentlemen' who came to live in the village. His brother Samuel Wade (1806-1878) built Ivy House.

On the other side of Uttoxeter Road stands the new (1929) Nag's Head. In the last few years the Nag's Head has been refurbished more than once and is now a modern eating place with a bar.

Further down Uttoxeter Road towards Derby is a hill area known as the Heights of Alma named after the Crimean War battle in 1854 in which the French and the British defeated the Russians.

The Mickleover Golf Club was officially formed in 1923. Land for the course and necessary buildings was let to the proposed club by the late Mr Harold Salt. The picture captions tell a few details about the golf club but it would require much more space that is available here to relate the improvements and changes made in recent years.

The construction work for the new A38 trunk road forced the old golf club members to play on a temporary nine-hole course. When this road was completed, the golf club moved over the road to their new clubhouse and eighteen-hole course. The new clubhouse is of a distinctive design and was built near to what was the third green on the old course. It was officially opened by His Worship the Mayor of Derby, Councillor George Guest, on Saturday, November 18th, 1972. Since 1973 there have been many changes to the course and the clubhouse to cater for the rising membership.

The first section of these photographs all look back towards The Square.

On the left of this picture is the entrance to Limes Avenue (Fennel Street). Then towards the Square is the Nag's Head, then houses which included the Post Office.

A clearer view of the Nag's Head and still evidence that horses did much of the carrier work in the village.

Someone had a camera so everyone tumbled out of the Nag's Head to have their picture taken, joined by local children.

An early picture of the Post Office. Letters arrived at 4.40am each day and were dispatched at 8.40pm.

The Nag's Head has gone and Foster & Son have taken the space. No parking problems in The Square.

We are now looking from the wall and hedge on the right of the first picture of this section, towards New School which opened in 1881 for the older children in the village. In 1950 the school became the Junior Mixed and Infants School until 1957 when the pupils were moved to the new school in Vicarage Road.

The Post Office has now moved but the camera still holds a special fascination for Mickleover people.

The Vine Inn with the 'smithy' on the right. The Derbyshire Building Society now has a branch office there.

The Post Office again. Could that be Mr Freckleton outside his new shop?

Did Mr Haines come before Mr Freckleton? Perhaps one of the little girls might let us know.

This section is looking from the Station Road Junction towards Derby city centre

Mickleover Lodge, which was built in the 1820s for Mr George Wade.

The Nag's Head was the second building to have that name and was taken over in 1929 by the tenants, Mr and Mrs Hinckley who had moved from the old Nag's Head.

A view from just below Mickleover Lodge looking towards Derby.

The section of the main Derby-Mickleover road called the Heights of Alma after a battle in the Crimean War.

This picture is looking back towards Mickleover to the Heights of Alma and on the right is the section between Cavendish Way and Arundel Avenue which is now completely built upon. On the left of the picture is the edge of the old Mickleover Golf Club.

A view of the old Mickleover Golf Course with the club house in the distance. This area is now covered by the houses on both sides of Brierfield Way.

A closer look at the old Club House — in 1951. For golfers' information the entrance fee for gentlemen was £4.4s.0d and the annual subscriptions were for ladies £4.4s.0d and gentlemen £5.5s.0d. If you were a visiting player it cost at that time 2s.6d per round, 3s.6d per day, Monday to Friday but 5s.0d on Saturdays, Sundays and Bank Holidays.

The Great Northern Railway

CONSTRUCTION of the Great Northern Railway commenced in 1875 and trains started running three years later, in 1878.

'Down' trains ran from Mickleover via Egginton to Burton and Stafford. 'Up' trains ran from Mickleover via Derby Friar Gate to Nottingham and Grantham.

The station at Mickleover was situated in a cutting adjacent to Mackworth Road (now Station Road), the road being carried over a railway cutting by a high brick arched bridge built on a slight skew. Adjacent to the bridge is the Great Northern Hotel which is another popular eating house and 'local'.

The line from Derby Friar Gate to Mickleover climbed steadily at a gradient of 1 in 100 into a quarter-of-a-mile tunnel before emerging near Station Road. Mickleover Station became known as 'Mickleover for Radbourne'.

The main purpose of the line was to carry freight, but with the capability of a modest passenger service. In 1887, Mickleover had a passenger service of 17 trains every day. By 1910, this had increased to 27 trains (30 on Saturdays).

The timetables allowed six minutes between Mickleover and Derby Friar Gate and vice versa.

There was a limiting factor of how much freight could be carried depending on how much one engine could pull up the bank from Derby. Many a freight train came to grief in or around Mickleover Tunnel and the station pilot engine from Friar Gate was regularly called upon to render rear assistance.

The year 1923 saw the multitude of different railway companies in the country reduced to four (London & North Eastern Railway, London Midland & Scottish, Great Western Railway and Southern Railway). Thus, the Great Northern Railway became part of the LNER. The growth in road traffic in the 1930s caused the Mickleover line to run at a loss and passenger trains had been reduced to seven trains in each direction.

World War Two strained the availability of staff at Mickleover Station. Before then there was a stationmaster, clerk, two porters and three signalmen. By the end of the war this had shrunk to one porter/clerk and three signalwomen. Services through Mickleover ceased in 1968 but the track between Egginton and Mickleover was used until recently by British Railways Research Department. The track has now been lifted.

Station Road

THE START THIS TIME is from Mickleover Station and up Station Road into the village. This area by the station was also the location of one of the main 'navvy' camps while the line was being built. A brickyard also existed on a site adjacent to the station before the line was constructed. When house building in Mickleover increased, the brickyard was enlarged and by 1912 it was known as the Station Brickworks. In 1879 the Mickleover & Etwall Gas Light and Coke Company was formed in order to bring the benefits of gas lighting to the two villages in its title.

Mickleover Station was 1¼ miles distance from the centre of the village. Many excursions were made to the East Coast from the station and it was described as being 'a very picturesque little wayside halt, with a primrose covered bank'. The country lanes of Goosecroft Road and Mackworth Road became known as Station Road.

The convenience of having such transport nearby meant that many new residents were attracted to the road. Large villas with spacious gardens, and some smaller houses were built along the tree-lined thoroughfare. In recent years the area close to the station, which had been used for railway freight, has been developed for smaller firms. At present some of the Rolls-Royce training is taking place where once Nestles and Keiller worked.

Nearer the village, many community activities began. In 1914 the new chapel was built on Station Road to replace a Wesleyan Chapel that was no longer capable of housing the growing congregation. The Methodists, Primitive, Wesleyan and United became united in 1932 and the chapel became the Methodist Church of Mickleover. The additions of an Assembly Hall and Sunday School were built in 1956, and in 1968 the church was modernised yet again.

After World War One it was decided that a community hall of some kind was needed for the village. A generous gift by Mr A. Preston Jones of Mickleover House enabled the purchase of a building which became known as 'the Memorial Hut'. The building was bought from the YMCA who had been using it at Derby's Midland Station. The YMCA provided aid and refreshments to any servicemen travelling during the war. A site was prepared on Station Road by a group of Mickleover volunteers of all ages and conditions. The 'Hut', as it is affectionately known today, accommodates a branch of the Derbyshire Library Service.

The rooms at the rear of the building are used by a variety of clubs.

The 'Mickleover for Radbourne' Station in its heyday when there were several trains to Derby each day.

The village windmill was moved from 'Mill Field' to Mickleover Common to a site just off Station Road when the Derbyshire Pauper Lunatic Asylum (Pastures Hospital) was built in 1852. This has now been covered by a housing development in the early 1970s, fronted by Onslow Road.

Looking back down Station Road from half way to the village.

Nearer the village centre but looking towards Mickleover Station.

A similar view to the previous photograph and clearer. The gentleman and young girl would not be standing there long with today's traffic.

The same view down the road as the last two pictures but a little earlier date judging by the hedge and tree growth and the missing telegraph poles.

Looking back again down Station Road. Note the bus and there are pavements on both sides of the road.

Looking up to the village now but back to one side of pavement only.

One pavement again but a good photograph of the 'corner shop' at the junction with Park Road.

A more modern look down from the village towards Mickleover Station. The corner shop has sunblinds and there is lighting on the road. Universal lighting came to the village in 1932.

A new Wesleyan Church was built on Station Road in 1914 and this group of the congregation came to celebrate the event.

The interior of the Church as it was before 1968.

'The Workers' — volunteers at the building of the Memorial Hut.

Vicarage Road

VICARAGE ROAD eventually ended up with this name after a few changes during the years. It has had various names during the last few centuries, the earliest recorded being Cackle Hill which was from the Old English 'caecca' or hump. Later maps show Cackle Hill changing into Cattle Hill. One Ordnance Survey map of an early date shows the name as Holly-end Street, and Park Road, which is the linking road from Vicarage Road to Station Road, was once called Holly-end Road.

Since the vicarage was built on the corner overlooking The Square at the top of the hill, the name change seems more appropriate.

The vicarage was a most impressive Regency house and the Revd Frederick Emanuel Hippolyte Curzon built the new vicarage, although it was an extravagance he could ill afford. Behind this elegant house and down Vicarage Road stood Cackle Hill Farm. The farm that stands there now has a field to the rear of it which is used for an annual small fair.

The more modern building development began in this road just before World War Two. The fields had been sold when Mickleover Manor changed hands and the houses were built opposite some older cottages and stand today.

Vicarage Road meanders down towards Park Road where a new medical centre has been erected. Park Road has an interesting past, too. In 1852, a building capable of holding 100 people and costing £100 was erected on Park Road by the Primitive Methodists. It is sited opposite The Dovedales which is a block of flats built in 1986. The outline of the original chapel sign and small windows in the brick structure, which is now a private house, can just be made out today.

There is not much more of historical note down Vicarage Road from the medical centre. To the left, as you follow the road, there is a small recreational park. The whole area is now built up with post-war housing on either side of the road. There are two shops on the right-hand side before the road curves left and ends at the junction with Fenton Road.

The Reverend Bindley stands in the doorway of the vicarage about 1920. The building was on the corner of Vicarage Road and Uttoxeter Road. On this site now are modern flats for the elderly.

This picture is of some early residents in their childhood standing at the top of Vicarage Road looking down the short hill. In the distance behind the boys are the houses near The Square on Uttoxeter Road.

This photograph seems to have been taken from almost where the children are standing in the previous photograph. There have been many pictures taken of this type of cart on this road.

A view taken from the cottage The cottage door and the buildings opposite can be identfied today.

As you can see, it's the same cottage with some residents standing in the road, but now the road is called Cattle Hill on the postcard bearing this picture.

This is a later photograph of the cottage. The building opposite is interesting too.

These two pictures show the changes from the old to the new. Parts of the old wall are still evident and the house windows and chimneys have not changed very much.

Before and after the building of the Vicarage Road Medical Centre.

New houses rise up in Vicarage Road, but there are still no pavements.

Western Road

WESTERN ROAD was originally known as Poke Lane and was built up when land was sold by the Wade family in the early 1900s. The road continues in a route parallel with Uttoxeter Road. A great deal of housing development took place along this road just before World War One. The building programme for this part of the village has continued over the years and now there is little land available in this area. Once again the larger villas were built first and then along the length of the road there were smaller properties built just before World War Two.

The few small shops along the road have been there for some time. Some of the larger villas have been adapted for uses other than as private homes.

The British Legion, which used to meet at the Nag's Head, moved to Western Road in 1939, to a large villa purchased from a Mr Eyre. The sports field of six acres adjoining the property was purchased with funds raised by gymkhanas. The field is still used for all kinds of meetings and also an annual May Day celebration. The Legion still is a social centre for many residents.

After World War Two there was another flourish of house building by Wimpey's which began with Brisbane Road and continued the development that trailed across the fields ending with Onslow Road and back on to Station Road. In particular the Australian names of the roads and closes added another interesting feature to Mickleover village.

The side roads from Western Road continue with house building on both sides. At the curved right turn in this road that leads to Uttoxeter Road is a left turn into Chevin Avenue. This avenue is the entrance to what used to be the Bishop Lonsdale Training College, but is now part of the University of Derby. The sports facilities and the swimming pool are excellent and at some arranged times local people can have use of the pool.

The houses on Western Road are easily identified by roof lines and the interesting shaped roof to a particular garage.

A view showing the opposite side of the road but once again the gable of the house can be seen clearly.

Further along the road on the right side but showing the lack of paving and no evidence of telegraph wiring.

Note the differences in the road surfaces and pavement edges of this taken from the opposite side of the road.

Two interesting pictures of the little cottage which stood near the end of Western Road as it bends towards Uttoxeter Road. The tree on the right presents the evidence for the dating sequence. They look a wonderful couple and the road surface is a little tidier in the second photograph.

A more recent picture of the remodelled cottage helps identify the pictures above.

Devonshire Drive from the Western Road end.

This picture shows an early view of West Drive, off Station Road, with empty fields at the end of the line of houses.

This picture gives an early view of East Avenue, off Station Road, and the tree in the middle of the road. The only clue to the date are the lack of television aerials.

Etwall Road

ALL SAINTS' CHURCH is usually believed to have been built after an older church on the site was destroyed by fire. The building of the church is reputed to be during the period of 1310-30. Much restorative rebuilding was done in 1858-59 but the original 14th-century font was removed and a Victorian font took its place. The old font spent some years in a neighbouring garden before it was returned. In 1951 it was restored to its former place inside the church.

Church registers began on 3 May 1607. During the last 50 years a vestry and organ chamber were built on the north side; the organ was rebuilt; a new choir vestry was brought into use on Christmas Eve 1965 and the Lady Chapel was consecrated in June 1967.

The clock was installed by John Smith in 1895 and since most of the village was on the south side of the church and the Manor House on the west, only two faces for the clock were deemed necessary. There were only open fields to the north and east so there was no need for a clock facing those directions.

Towards Etwall and situated close to the church is Mickleover Manor which was part of the estate bought by Mr Newton in the 17th century. The house was completely rebuilt in the 18th century and remained with the Newton family until the present century.

Mickleover Manor has been described as a 'neo Tudor structure with shaped gables and mullioned and transomed windows'. There were reputed to be 70 windows in the building which indicated a rich owner. Until World War One, some member of the Newton family lived there but at the end of the war they moved to Lockington Hall after the death of Francis Curzon Newton. Sir Frederick and Lady Inglefield lived at the Manor for several years and then the house was let. This time with a complete change of use, from a home to a private preparatory school for boys aged five to 14. The school advertised a sportsmanlike type of life for the boys, in healthy surroundings. An open-air swimming pool was built and the house was rearranged to accommodate the pupils. The school closed in 1950.

There was a change of name to Woodlands Hospital when the buildings were taken over to house patients of the Health Authority. That closed in 1989 and the house is currently being converted in new homes with further houses being built in the grounds.

A splendid new hotel, the Mickleover Court, has opened by the roundabout on Etwall Road. It is built to an interesting design and is attracting many new visitors to the area.

In the early days, the farm lands followed the line of the road until the coming of the Derbyshire Pauper Lunatic Asylum (1851), known later as Pastures Hospital. The decision to build on Mill Field must have created a great change and many problems for villagers. One of the major upheavals was the removal of the Mill and rebuilding it nearer the railway.

Into their community came patients from all over the county and the attendant hospital staff. It was a model hospital and used as an example of good practice for other counties. The chains that had restrained the patients were removed and they were amazed at the new regime. Kindness and nursing had not been part of their lives before.

The hospital became an almost self supporting community with farming playing a large part. The patients were encouraged to work at suitable tasks. Before the 19th century ended the hospital housed 20 wards, having approximately 500 patients. There were many changes to the buildings before the end of the century. A chapel was built and various workrooms to encourage the patients to work as part of their treatment. There was sewing, laundry and baking for female patients and tailoring, beer-house work, shoemaking, gardening and farming for the men.

There was a great effort to include the hospital in the life of the village. In recent years a nine-hole golf course was made and many hospital staff and local people became members.

This hospital is now closed and as yet no firm decision seems to have been taken regarding the future. There are still many houses adjoining the old hospital and also a very popular garden centre is flourishing nearby.

Mickleover All Saints Church stands back from the road and is fronted by a Memorial Cross to remind us of the people who gave their lives in the past wars.

A 1909 picture of the south side of All Saints' Church.

The interior of All Saints' Church, for many years a focal point of the village community.

Mickleover Manor, described in 1857 as 'the ancient seat of the Newtons'.

Mickleover Manor from the rear showing the house's extensive gardens.

The main door at Mickleover Manor.

The swimming pool at Mickleover Manor School.

The rear of the cottage which faced the site of what is now the Mickleover Court Hotel. It stood on the corner which was on the Etwall Old Road opposite the entrance to Mickleover Manor.

Pastures Hospital

Building started in 1849 and the hospital opened in 1851 with 300 beds in 12 wards. Known originally as the Derbyshire Pauper Lunatic Asylum, its patients came from Union Workhouses all over the county to be treated at Mickleover.

Designed by Henry Duesbury, this view shows the remarkable array of five-dome capped towers, four-towered central pavilion and varied roof line, seen here around 1900.

The main entrance to hospital.

An excellent aerial view of Pastures Hospital showing the vast area covered by wards and the various buildings that were put up as part of the treatment for the patients. A chapel was built and the men worked on the farm. Later a brass band was formed and the large main hall in the hospital was used for many functions and dances. The hospital operated its own laundry and bakehouse.

The Lodge at Pastures Hospital, pictured in 1935.

Orchard Street

THE SQUARE and Limes Avenue (Fennel Street) have already been discussed. These three remaining areas link with those two in being at the heart of 'old' Mickleover and near All Saints' Church.

Orchard Street is almost opposite the church and leads down from Etwall Road. The oldest house in Mickleover is The Old Hall which was originally called The Cedars. The Old Hall is a well preserved half-timbered house of red bricks and black oak beams. In the porch above the door is carved the inscription *'Ni deus frustra 1648'* (In vain but for God). The house was built for William Cotchett who died in 1635, leaving the building to his son Robert Cotchett (1611-1657), who supported the Parliamentarians. There are stories that Oliver Cromwell stayed at the The Cedars when Tutbury Castle was under attack. It is still possible to identify cedar trees in various gardens around. Those trees must have been part of the original estate.

The Old Hall was let and changed hands many times in the years that followed until 1830 when it was bought by Moses Harvey. It cost £900 to be 'repaired and beautified' according to *Bagshaw's History, Gazetteer and Directory* for 1846.

At about the same time a field adjoining The Cedars was sold and Mickleover House built in 1824 for Alderman Samuel Rowland. The house is now much altered but still stands today beside one of the cedars. Mickleover House is now a nursing home. Another large old house called Overfields, accessed by a hidden drive, was built very near Mickleover House. Overfields is now a residential home.

Turning the corner at the bottom of Orchard Street the narrow street known as The Green lies ahead. This collection has no old photographs of The Green, although there are some pleasing old cottages and houses along there. It was also an area involved with religion in Mickleover when a Wesleyan Chapel was built on The Green in 1820. The building was later used by Mickleover School as a handicraft room.

Old documents suggest that the name The Green referred to the large drying area used by villagers. When some old trees had to be removed, hooks were found embedded in their trunks. It is known that on The Green some beautiful pillow lace was made in one of the cottages.

At the junction of The Green with The Hollow stands Ivy House and on the other side of The Hollow is a 16th-century timber-framed house. Ivy House is a relatively modern house, built by Samuel Wade (1806-1878). However in the cellar is a stone built into the wall with the initials 'G.W. 1694'.

On The Hollow there are a number of old properties and some newer buildings. The trough near the bottom of The Hollow would have been used in the past as a water source for the poorer homes as well as refreshment for the horses. Ribbons and blankets were woven in a small house in The Hollow. Legend has it that there was a secret passage linking Mickleover Hall with Mickleover Old Hollow Cottage. The Hollow used to be a through road but became much too dangerous with modern traffic. The new Brookfield Primary School was built at the bottom of The Hollow after it was closed to traffic.

One of the original buildings in Orchard Street. It still stands today.

The Old Hall — the earliest photograph Mr Short had in his collection.

The original carving above the door of The Old Hall '*Nisi Deus Frustra 1648*' (In vain but for God). It was probably put there when Richard Cotchett returned home after the Civil War.

A more modern photograph of entrance to The Old Hall (The Cedars).

In the late 1830s, Mickleover House was built on a field bought from the owners of The Old Hall.

The Lodge and drive down to Overfield House.

The Hollow

This scene in The Hollow is from the early 1900s judging by the suits and walking sticks.

A postcard view of the top of The Hollow in Mickelover.

The south face of Ivy House which is a relatively modern house, built on an old foundation.

Looking down The Hollow.

Further down the hill.

When delivering groceries, The Hollow was quite a push for a cyclist.

Further down the hill near the old trough. Again, the camera has attracted many local children.

Limes Avenue

The right-hand side of Limes Avenue, originally known as Fennel Street.

An old picture showing both sides of Limes Avenue from the top.

A modern, if distant, picture of The Limes which is now a residential home.

Miscellany

I N V E N T O R Y

&

V A L U A T I O N

OF FIXTURES, FITTINGS, TRADE UTENSILS AND STOCK

IN TRADE   AT

"T H E   N A G S   H E A D   I N N"

MICKLEOVER,   DERBYSHIRE.

From:- Mr.Frederick Storer.

To:-   Mr.Edward Hinkley.

License, Rates & Inhabited House Duty adjusted

to date.

OCTOBER 9th. 1923.

Amount of Valuation :- ONE HUNDRED AND FORTY ONE

POUNDS, ONE SHILLING AND ELEVEN PENCE

(£141-1-11).

Valuers for both parties:-

RICHARDSON & LINNELL.
AUCTIONEERS & VALUERS,
DERBY.

The valuation notice for the transfer of innkeeper in October 1923. From Mr Storer to Mr Hinkley

Smith's Tea Rooms — they used to be situated on Etwall Road almost opposite the War Memorial.

Outside the Vine Inn — a family outing!

Somewhere on Staker Lane? Anyone know the girl?

The Mickleover Brass Band. Perhaps the trumpter was probably still waiting for his uniform to be altered.

An early school picture — it looks like All Saints' Church in the background.

Another early picture – a pity the schoolmistress is only partially seen.

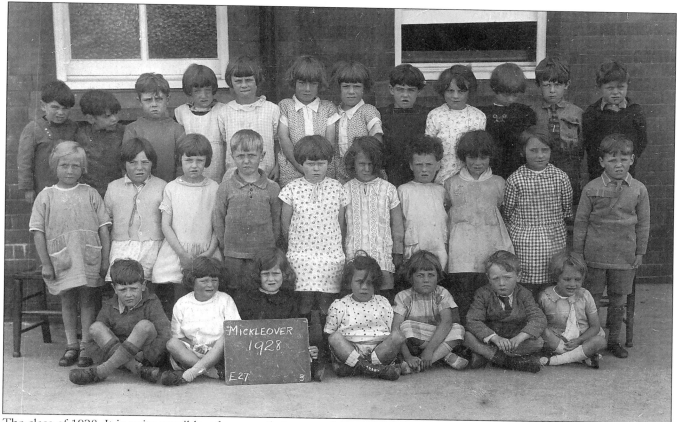

The class of 1928. It is quite possible, of course, that some of these children are now adult residents of Mickleover.

A more modern picture of a Mickleover School class.

Bibliography

The Story of Mickleover and its Church	V.H. Brix
The Mickleover Story	Ford & Ravensdale
Mickleover and Littleover – a history	Susan Watson
History, Gazetteer and Directory of Derbyshire	Bagshaw, 1846
Mickleover Golf Club Official Handbooks	1951/1958/1973
The Friargate Line	Mark Higginson
The Illustrated History of Derby's Suburbs	Maxwell Craven